GOAL SETTING SKILLS for YOUNG ADULTS

Success from Goals

Second Edition

Bettie B. Youngs, Ph.D., Ed.D.

𝓅
Jalmar Press
Torrance, California

Goal Setting Skills for Young Adults
• *Success from Goals*

© Copyright 1995, Bettie B. Youngs, Ph.D., Ed.D.

All rights reserved. No part of this book may be reproduced or transmitted in any form by any means, electronic or mechanical, including photocopying and recording, or by any information storage or retrieval system, except as may be expressly permitted by the 1976 Copyright Act or in writing by the publisher. Request for such permission should be addressed to:

>Jalmar Press
>Attn: Permissions Dept.
>2675 Skypark Drive, Suite 204
>Torrance, CA 90505-5330
>310/784-0016 or Fax 310/784-1379

Published by Jalmar Press

Goal Setting Skills for Young Adults
• *Goals for Success*

Author: Bettie B. Youngs, Ph.D., Ed.D.
Editor: Susan Remkus
Project Director: Jeanne Iler
Design and Make-up: Electronic Publishing Services, Inc.

Manufactured in the United States of America
Second Edition: Printing: 10 9 8 7 6 5 4 3 2 1
ISBN: 1-880396-33-5

GOAL SETTING SKILLS for YOUNG ADULTS

Success from Goals

Second Edition

JP
Jalmar Press

About the Author

Bettie B. Youngs, Ph. D., Ed.D. is an author, counselor and consultant to schools nation-wide. Her work has spanned more than 60 countries for more than two decades, earning her a reputation as a respected authority in the field of personal and professional development. She has earned national acclaim for her work on the effects of stress on health, wellness and productivity for both adults and children, and for her work on the role of self-esteem as it detracts from or empowers vitality, achievement and peak performance.

Dr. Youngs is a former Teacher-of-the Year, Professor at San Diego State University, and Executive Director of the Phoenix Foundation. Currently she is President of Bettie B. Youngs & Associates, and senior consultant with Instruction & Professional Development, Inc. Dr. Youngs is the author of 14 books published in 23 languages, as well as a number of popular audio cassette programs.

As a member of the National Speakers Association, Dr. Youngs addresses audiences throughout the U.S. and abroad, meeting with nearly 250,000 youth and adults each year. She serves on the Board of Directors for the National Counsel for Self-Esteem, and is a frequent guest on radio and television talk shows.

To contact Dr. Youngs:

Bettie B. Youngs & Associates
Instructions & Professional Development, Inc.
3060 Racetrack View Drive
Del Mar, CA 92014
(619) 481-6360

Other Works By Bettie B. Youngs

Books

Stress and Your Child: Helping Kids Cope with the Stress, Strains, and Pressures of Life (New York: Randon House)

How to Develop Self-Esteem In Your Child: 6 Vital Ingredients (New York: Macmillan/Fawcett)

Keeping Our Children Safe: A Parent's Guide to Emotional, Physical, Intellectual and Spiritual Wellness (Louisville, Kentucky: Westminister/John Knox Press)

Safeguarding Your Teenager From the Dragons of Life: A Guide to the Adolescent Years (Deerfield Beach, Florida: Health Communications)

Is Your Net-Working? A Complete Guide to Building Contacts and Career Visibility (New York: John Wiley & Sons)

A Stress Management Guide For Young People (Rolling Hills Estates, CA: Jalmar Press)

Problem Solving Skills for Children, Ages 3-10 (Rolling Hills Estates, CA: Jalmar Press)

Getting Back Together: Creating a New Relationship With Your Partner and Making It Last (New York: Bob Adams, Inc.)

Self-Esteem for Educators: It's Job Criteria #1 (Rolling Hills Estates, CA: Jalmar Press)

You and Self-Esteem: A Book for Young People (Grade 5-12) (Rolling Hills Estates, CA: Jalmar Press)

Stress Management Guide for Educators: A Guide to Manage Your Response to Stress (Rolling Hills Estates, CA: Jalmar Press)

A Stress Management Guide for Administrators (Rolling Hills Estates, CA: Jalmar Press)

Friendship is Forever, Isn't It? (Rolling Hills Estates, CA: Jalmar Press)

The 6 Vital Ingredients of Self-Esteem and How to Develop Them in Your Students (Rolling Hills Estates, CA: Jalmar Press)

Stories from The Heartland: A Book of Principles, Values and Other Worthy Ideals (Deerfield Beach, Florida: Health Communication, 1995)

Audio Cassettes

Helping The Teenager Deal With Stress (Health Communications)

How to Raise Happy, Healthy, Self-Confident Children (Nightengale/Conant)

The 6 Vital Components of Self-Esteem (Sybervision)

Helping Children Manage Anxiety, Pressure, and Stress (Sybervision)

Getting Back Together (Sybervision)

Developing Responsibility in Children (Sybervision)

Table Of Contents

Introduction

Chapter 1

Who is in Charge of Your Life? — 1

Why Setting Goals Is Important — 1
There Are Alternatives to Living by Accident — 2
Identifying Your Goals — 3
Identifying Obstacles to Goals — 4
It's Up to You — 6
Exercise 1. Understanding Where You Are Right Now — 7
Exercise 2. Getting Where You Want to Go — 8
Exercise 3. Failure Isn't Fatal — 9

Chapter 2

Keys to Goal Setting — 10

Life Is a "Do-It-Yourself" Project — 10
Focus on Your Area of Excellence — 10
Finding What You Are Good At? — 11
Locating Your "Acres of Diamonds" — 12
Have a Number One Goal — 13
Exercise 1. Identifying Your "Acres of Diamonds" — 14
Exercise 2. Finding Your Area of Excellence — 15
Exercise 3. Determining Your Number One Goal — 16

Chapter 3

Set Yourself Up for Success — 18

Six Steps to Goal Setting — 18
Rewarding Yourself — 23
Exercise 1. What's Important to YOU? — 23
Exercise 2. Evaluating Your Goal — 25
Exercise 3. Setting Subgoals — 26

Chapter 4

Overcoming Obstacles to Achieving Goals — 27

Six Steps on the Path to Success — 27
Exercise 1. Accomplishing Your Goal — 30
Exercise 2. Overcoming Obstacles — 32

Chapter 5

The Keys to Success — 33

The Six Keys to Success — 33
Exercise 1. Defining Success For YOU — 36
Exercise 2. Goals for YOUR Success — 38

Appendices

Daily Goals Worksheet
Weekly Goals Worksheet

Introduction

Answer this question: ***What do you want?*** Your first response was probably very simple: I want to be HAPPY, POPULAR, and SUCCESSFUL.

What a great answer! That's exactly what most of us want. It's perfectly natural to want to be happy, to be liked and respected by others, and to be successful. But now comes an even bigger question: HOW can you BECOME happy, popular, and successful?

One very important way is to set GOALS and work toward them. A plan for being happy, popular, and successful, for working toward something you really want, helps you actually get it. You have seen this happen in your own life in many ways. Perhaps you wanted a new cassette tape or CD, and did extra chores to earn money for it. The cassette or CD was your goal; doing the chores was your plan. Without a plan, you could have daydreamed forever, but you would never have received your tape or CD. To turn your wants and dreams into accomplished goals, you needed to take ACTION.

And that's what this book is about. In **Goal Setting Skills for Young Adults**, we'll be looking at:

- Why goals are important
- How to identify your goals
- Keys to goal setting (how to get started)
- Steps to goal setting (actually creating interesting and achievable goals)
- Rewarding yourself for accomplishing your goals
- Overcoming obstacles to reaching your goals
- Keys to success (how to get the most out of your life)

This book will help you to think about what you want most, and to take steps toward those goals. You will find two to three exercises at the end of each chapter. Each exercise is designed to reinforce what you learned, and to help you apply the information to your own life. The book also features appendices of additional worksheets you can use. These include:

- Daily goal statements
- Weekly goal statements
- Monthly goal statements

(You may want to create additional worksheets, on your own. Great! Put them here, in the appendices.)

Remember, an exciting and rewarding life rarely occurs by chance. Success and happiness can be planned for, and the best time to begin is right now. So, if you're ready to start thinking about what is truly important to you personally, if you're ready to make plans to have a great life, if you're ready to take control over your own future, let's get started! Here's to helping you become everything you ever wanted to be and helping you get what you want!

What others say about this book!

"At first I thought that setting goals was just another exercise, something ELSE to do. But when I put my goals in writing, I could see what was important to me, and why I should devote more time and attention to those things and be careful that I didn't waste too much time on other things that really weren't all that important in the long run."

Tonya Williams, 11th grade

"So often I feel that there just isn't enough time to do all the things I want to do. This book showed me how to prioritize the things I wanted to do. It's not about time, it's about doing the right things!"

Rick Torres, 10th grade

"Setting goals helps me to do those things that I really want to accomplish. This workbook became a very useful tool for me to make sure I stick to those things I want to achieve."

Lisa Harmon, 12th grade

"Setting goals is the one way to make sure that you are going to get where you want to go."

John Thomas, 7th grade

"This comprehensive workbook written for young people themselves, shows them how setting goals can lead to achievement and personal satisfaction. This book is their "personal coach" in turning wishful thinking into a plan of action. A must for all young people."

Susan Hendricks, Educator, Brandt Secondary School

"Young people need assistance in formulating realistic goals and evaluating their importance in terms of moving them toward where they want to go. This resource helps young people learn how to remove obstacles that prevent them from accomplishing their goals, and empowers them to believe in themselves in being successful in what they want to achieve."

Beth Muldune, Educator, Lincoln High School

"This book is a valuable tool in changing wishful thinking into goal achievement. I use this workbook as a complete goal-setting course. Good stuff!"

Thomas Sharitt, Counselor, Smithton Middle School

Chapter 1

Who is in Charge of Your Life?

Are you *managing* your life? Are YOU shaping the direction of your life? Or, are you letting others do it? Are YOU in charge?

You know, some young people feel as though they have little say in their lives. Many teens believe that parents, teachers, friends, and others have more to do with what happens to them than they themselves do. If that's true for you, too, then you are assigning a lot of responsibility to others for the events in your life. That can make you feel powerless. Feeling powerless is not a good feeling. **This book will help you see just how powerful you can be in shaping the events in your life, and will teach you how to get what you want out of life. Setting goals is the key.**

Why Setting Goals Is Important

Why are goals important? Goals help you PLAN what you want to have happen in your life. If you just go along letting life happen to you, you'll have no idea what's going to occur next. It could be something wonderful... but then again, it could be something that you don't want to have happen. When you cannot predict what's going to happen to you, things may not turn out the way you'd like them to. You may fail to accomplish anything worthwhile. You may never get what YOU want.

To put it another way: Failing to plan is planning to fail. If you fail to study that difficult material in your history class, you may not be able to pass a test on it. Or to use a sports analogy, suppose that you are going to run a mile race. If you don't plan by eating the right foods, getting into shape, and warming up before the race, if you just tumble out of bed that morning saying brightly, "Gee, I wonder how I am going to do in this race today!" you will do poorly. Plus, you just might feel awful when you are through, assuming you do finish! Another example: If you don't plan a meal but just raid the refrigerator instead, you might end up having whipped cream and sardines for breakfast! Or if you don't plan what you are going to wear, you might get up one morning and find that all your clothes are dirty, and all you have to wear is a ski parka and shorts! Now, those are obviously silly examples, but they do illustrate how important it is to make plans in life.

There Are Alternatives to Living by Accident

When you make a plan, you take control of your life by shaping it—by charting a course of direction. Having a plan is like having a blueprint or a map to get where you're going. Winners constantly take advantage of this fact. The difference between winners and losers, between those who achieve and those who don't, is that **successful people are *proactive*—they actively decide what THEY want out of life, and then make a plan and follow that plan.** THEY direct their lives. Unsuccessful people, on the other hand, just let life happen by accident, without being in charge of planning it.

Identifying Your Goals

Can you identify your goals? You might be thinking of a short-term goal, like getting through today without getting called on because you didn't do your homework! Or you might have a long-term goal, like getting a CD player, having a phone line of your own, or saving money to buy a car. Whatever your goals are, you need to be able to state them clearly so that you can make a plan for accomplishing them.

There was an interesting study made of students at Yale a few years ago. Now, students at Yale are some of the most skilled, academically gifted, motivated students around. A researcher asked whether they had specific, *written* goals. Out of all of those students, only about 3 percent had specific, written, well-thought-out goals. Years later, a follow-up study was done on those same students. It turned out that the 3 percent who had set specific written goals were doing better, were making more money, were more successful and happier, than the entire other 97 percent! Why? Because they had a focus for their intelligence and skills and they knew where they were going. Think of this as two drivers. One driver has a goal, a destination. He starts off and drives straight towards that goal, and in due time gets there. The other driver has no goal, no destination. He takes off... and goes in circles. He drives around and around and around, spinning his car's wheels, using up gas and oil, never getting anywhere. Note that it makes no difference where the two drivers start from. The same is true of you. Don't worry if your friends don't share the same goals you do. If you have goals you are on your way to getting what you want out of life.

Identifying Obstacles to Goals

Why isn't everyone an ace goal setter? Why don't people talk more about goals? Why don't you and your friends draw up contracts to work toward your goals, saying that you will learn a new dance before the prom, actively explore all your options for selecting an interesting career, or vow that you will get a better grade on the next exam? In other words, what are the obstacles to goal setting? What are the reasons—or rather the excuses!—that people use to avoid being in charge of their lives?

OBSTACLES TO GOAL SETTING

1. "Goals Aren't All That Important."

Some people don't realize the importance of goal setting. Let's face it, you and your friends don't sit around the lunch table and say, "Gee, I think we should all set goals because they are soooo important!" The topic of goals, quite probably, has never come up. Notice how many young people feel out of control of their own lives. After all, if you think someone else controls your life, why bother to set goals for yourself? Of course, you know that no matter how things seem right now, you are ultimately responsible for your own life. YOU are in charge of YOU.

2. "I Don't Know How."

How many courses have you had in goal setting? Probably not too many. Some young people say the reason they don't set goals is because they just don't know how. This is like saying the reason you don't build your own bicycle from scratch, or repair a car, is because you don't know how. Sure, it would be great to be able to go down to the junk yard, pick up a few pieces here and there, and create a bicycle for almost nothing, rather than having to go to the store and spend $200 or more for that same bicycle. But if you don't know how to put together a bike, you have to pay the price for not knowing. The same is true with goals. If you don't know how to create or set a goal, you pay the price. The good news is that goal setting is not difficult (or expensive!).

3. "What If Someone Makes Fun of My Goal?"

The third reason some people don't make goals is fear of being criticized. Suppose your goal is to lose 10 pounds by the end of the year. You tell your best friend, and she says, "Oh, that's impossible. You can't do that. You're always trying to lose weight and you never do." Or maybe your goal is to be a starter on the basketball team. You tell your friend, who immediately snickers and says, "That team doesn't want you. It wants someone who's tall, who moves fast, and who has the ability to block. You're just wasting your time!" Things like this happen. Your friends, whether for a good reason or out of jealousy, often will put down your goals. Maybe those friends are concerned that if you achieve your goal, you will be more popular and not want to be around them anymore. Maybe those friends sincerely want to help you and are trying, in their opinion, to keep you from making a mistake or making a fool of yourself. Whatever the reason, people often criticize other people's goals. The solution is to share goals only with those who are supportive of you. This is especially true if your goal is a big one, like being the star player on the team when you are now second string, or losing 30 pounds when you have never dieted successfully before.

4. "I Might Fail!"

The fourth reason that some people don't set goals is the fear of failure. So what if you do fail? Thomas Edison didn't create the electric light bulb on the first try. Do you think he woke up one morning, said, "Today's goal is to create an electric light bulb," went into his lab and did so, presto? No, of course not. Edison failed, and failed, and failed. He made mistake after mistake, up to thousands of times. When an associate of his said to him, "You should give up. You have failed thousands of times," Edison made a wonderful reply. He looked at his associate and said, "No, I have not failed thousands of times. Instead, I have successfully eliminated thousands of ideas that do not work." What a great attitude! Edison didn't think of himself as a failure, but as someone who slowly but surely was successfully eliminating wrong options. Edison learned from every mistake. He wasn't afraid to fail, and thus he became one of the most important inventors of all time.

You shouldn't be afraid to fail, either. Life is about learning. Chances are, you've failed at a number of things. What have YOU learned from your failures? From every mistake, you learn something. From every disappointment, you become stronger. Suppose you get a D on an exam. What have you learned? That you need to study even harder the next time? If you let the fear of failure prevent you from setting goals, you are losing the power to shape your own life, to make it what YOU want it to be.

It's Up to You

Now that you recognize all the excuses for not setting goals, you can begin to put them behind you. It's time to begin setting some goals of your own. The first step is to get to know yourself a little better, to think about your life as it is now.

EXERCISE 1. *Understanding Where You Are Right Now*

1. How do you feel about yourself and your life right now? Are you in_____control, or are you just letting things happen? Explain. _____
   _{full, moderate, somewhat}
   _____

2. Think of a time when you had a goal and a plan, and worked toward that goal in an organized manner. Did you succeed on the first try? Explain. _____
   _____

3. Did you ever feel like giving up? If so, when? _____
   _____

4. List two areas of **your** life in which you feel you have control and confidence. ____
   _____
   _____
   _____

5. What are two areas of your life that you let operate by "accident"? (For example, you want to get good grades, but fail to do your homework. What are the chances of consistently getting good grades?) _____
   _____
   _____
   _____

EXERCISE 2. *Getting Where You Want to Go*

1. How can setting goals give you more *control* over your life? _____
   _____
   _____

2. How could you *improve your performance* by having a goal and a plan for achieving it? _____
   _____

3. Why would you be *happier* by having a goal and a plan for achieving it? _____
   _____

4. How does fear of being criticized affect the goals you set? _____
   _____

5. How can you overcome this fear? _____
   _____

6. How does the fear of failure affect the goals you set? _____
   _____
   _____

7. How can you overcome this fear? _____
   _____
   _____

Exercise 3. *Failure Isn't Fatal*

You can triumph over failure by learning from your mistakes. You can turn failure into success by learning from every setback. List two disappointments you have had and at least one valuable lesson you learned from each one.

Disappointment: _____
_____
_____
_____

Valuable Lesson: _____
_____
_____
_____

Disappointment: _____
_____
_____
_____

Valuable Lesson: _____
_____
_____
_____

Chapter 2

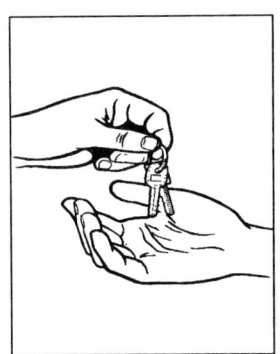

Keys to Goal Setting

Life Is a "Do-It-Yourself" Project

Life really IS a do-it-yourself project. Your parents and teachers provide protection and guidance. But, in the final analysis, what you make of yourself in life is up to you. This chapter is about helping you clarify what you are about, so that you can go about doing what you want to do. In the last chapter, you thought about where you are right now, about how your life is going. In this chapter, you are going to learn to match your strengths with your dreams, and to set a goal that is meaningful to you.

Focus on Your Area of Excellence

Everyone has something at which he or she excels. You might be good at acting, while your best friend is a strong athlete, and another friend finds math and science easy. Sometimes it takes a while to find those areas of excellence, but they are there. Why do you think you go to school and study so many different things? Not everyone is going to use the skills he or she learns in Biology class in the future, but everyone still has to be exposed to a Biology class. Why? One reason is so that everyone can find his or her area of expertise. The more things you are exposed to, the better your chances of finding what you are really good at. If you read the biographies of successful people, you will often find that there was one turning point in each person's life. For example, a dancer might have been taken to the ballet by her parents when she was just a child, and said, "That's it, that's what I want to do with my life." Or an actor may have taken an easy class in drama, just to get the credit. Then he discovered he had a talent for acting, and became a star. These things really do happen, but only because the individuals discovered what they had an interest in.

Finding What You Are Good At

In what areas should you set your goals? One key is discovering what captures your attention. You do better in those things that interest you than in those things that don't hold your interest. In Physical Education class, you might be good at volleyball because you like it. But how good are you at square dancing? If you don't want to dance, you might do so anyway because the teacher makes you, but you won't try very hard. And, of course, if you want to be successful you *have* to try very hard.

Have you ever been doing something and lost all track of time? Have you ever been involved in a project, and suddenly found that several hours had passed and you hadn't even realized it? We've all had that experience. Watch for the times when you are so absorbed or involved in a project that nothing else seems to matter. You are concentrating on that activity because it interests you. That means that you are probably good at it, or can become good at it.

NOTE: This does not mean you should stop working in subjects that are not your best. If you find History difficult, you still have to study for the tests and pass the class. I'm not suggesting that you say, "I never do well in this, so I may as well not waste any more time on it." That would be a great way for students to get out of learning Algebra or Biology, but you need to put effort into all areas. What I am saying, however, is that there will be **one** (or perhaps more than one) area in which you excel. Put *extra* time and effort into that area and the rewards will come.

Locating Your "Acres of Diamonds"

The second key to goal setting is the Acres of Diamonds Concept. A friend of mine illustrates this concept by telling the story about a farmer who got bored with farming and decided to seek his fortune in a gold mine. After selling his farm, he went to Alaska and searched for gold. He was gone many years and had all sorts of adventures. But he never did find gold, and he lived a very poor life, sometimes not having enough food, and never having a nice place to live. Finally, exhausted and out of hope, he traveled back to see his former farm, just for old times' sake. To his amazement, he found that a mansion stood where the farmhouse had been, and the grounds were gorgeous. The new owner came out to talk to the former farmer. "What on earth happened here?" asked the bewildered farmer. "You barely had enough money to buy the farm from me, as I remember. How did you get so rich?"

The new owner just smiled. "Actually, it was all due to you. There were diamonds on this property, acres and acres of diamonds!" The old farmer scoffed. "Diamonds! I knew every inch of this land, and there were no diamonds here." The new owner nodded, and pulled from his pocket a lump of what looked like coal. "I carry around this small one as a good luck charm. Here is one of the diamonds from this property."

The farmer was amazed. "That's a diamond? I remember seeing a lot of those all over this land. I used to swear at them and kick them because they got in the way when I was plowing. I thought they were lumps of coal! That doesn't look anything like a diamond to me!"

You see, the farmer sold perfectly good land that could have made him a millionaire, because he didn't recognize the diamonds when he saw them. Not all diamonds look like diamonds; in their unpolished form, they look like lumps of coal. You have diamonds in your life that YOU may not be recognizing right now. Something that seems worthless or silly might be extremely valuable. For example, if you have an ability to mimic people, you might think that is just a fun thing to do at parties—but maybe it's a sign that you have dramatic ability and could be a good actor, with practice. If you are able to explain things to your classmates, so that they are always asking you for help, you might think that you have a skill that is a pain in the neck, since others pester you a lot. However, that skill, with practice, could make you a good teacher, or professor, or consultant, or public speaker. The point of all this is to know that you have those "diamonds." You have to find them, then you have to work on polishing them so they look like the diamonds they really are.

Have a Number One Goal

You need to have a number one goal, a goal that you feel so strongly about that it is in your mind all the time. You'll find that this goal may be broad and general, like "I want to get into a good college," or "I want a car."

You can have a lot of different goals. In fact, you *need* a variety of goals for balance. How, then, can you decide on this number one goal? Ask yourself how much you want to reach it. If you very casually say, "Yes, I think I want to be a part of the soccer team this year," you are not very intense. But if you say, "I absolutely have to be on the soccer team, I'm going to do what it takes!" Wow! Are you intense! Remember that you work harder and with more enthusiasm toward goals that are important to you. If you want a number one goal, it should be something toward which you are willing to work very hard. You have probably heard stories of athletes who practice eight, ten, or more hours a day, giving up their social lives, spending every minute working on their sport. They do this because being the best at their sport is their number one goal, more important than anything else. These athletes have an intensity of purpose.

If you are not intense, you will not put in the necessary effort. If you do not put in the effort, you probably will fail. If you keep setting goals and not accomplishing them, soon you will be discouraged and quit, defeating your own purpose. Find something that is more important to you than anything else, and make that your number one goal.

EXERCISE 1. *Identifying Your "Acres of Diamonds"*

1. What subjects capture your *attention*? When you're looking for a book in the library, what do you pick up and read? What informational programs do you watch on television? What classes do you really enjoy? List them below.

   _____
   _____
   _____
   _____

2. What activities do you most enjoy *doing*? _____
   _____
   _____
   _____
   _____

3. When you feel completely *absorbed* in something, what you are doing?_____

   _____

   _____

4. Think of a time when you thought you had a "lump of coal," but you actually had a "diamond." Can you remember a time when you worked hard toward something, only to find that you had overlooked the obvious?

   _____

   _____

   _____

EXERCISE 2. *Finding Your Area of Excellence*

1. List skills you have in each area below. These skills can be major, or relatively minor. The goal of this exercise is to make you think of all the many talents and aptitudes you really have.

   Academic _____

   Social _____

   Family _____

   Athletic _____

   Artistic _____

   Literary _____

   Dramatic _____

   Other _____

2. Which of these skills do you consider your own personal "diamonds"? _____
   _____

EXERCISE 3. *Determining Your Number One Goal*

Write two goals you have in each of the areas listed below. Then, thinking carefully about all of them, come up with a Number One Goal, something that right now is the most important thing to you.

1. **Spiritual growth:** Goals for peace of mind, search for meaning, spiritual fulfillment. _____
   _____

2. **Personal relationships:** Goals in your relationships (with parents, friends, teachers, others). _____
   _____

3. **Learning/education:** What would you like to know more about? What skills do you want to develop? _____
   _____

4. **Status and respect:** Which groups do you want to belong to? From whom do you want respect? _____
   _____

5. **Leisure time:** What activities (hobbies, sports, travel) would you like to learn more about? To do more of? _____
   _____

6. **Fitness:** Goals for your physical fitness and overall health. _____
_____
_____

7. **Financial:** Goals for having enough money to do the things you want to do. _____
_____
_____

8. **Job/career:** What kind of job would you like? What are your goals for productive work and career success? _____
_____

9. **Others:** Goals that may not fit into the previous categories. _____
_____
_____

Now go back and select the one goal that is most important to you right now. Write it below.

#1 Goal: _____
_____

Why is this your most important goal? _____
_____

Chapter 3

Set Yourself Up for Success

Setting a goal is like having a map. It tells you where you should be heading. A goal directs where you should focus your time. By learning how to set goals now, you get a head start on success. You set a pattern to behave in a certain way. It's like walking a particular path to school. If you walk it often enough, it becomes a habit, and you can follow it without even thinking, knowing that it will lead you to your destination. If you learn how to formulate purposeful goals, you feel good about yourself, proud and confident, and you want to set goals again and again. Success in one area often leads to success in another area. That's the whole idea. But you have to make certain that your goals are realistic and obtainable. There are six steps that set the pattern to becoming a successful goal setter.

Six Steps to Goal Setting

1. Desire

You have to have a burning desire, a very strong motivation, to strive to get to where you want to go. If you don't really want a certain goal, it's not likely that you'll make the commitment to accomplish it, and you'll probably give up when faced with hard work. If you set goals that are too easy, you won't have a strong motivation to accomplish them. There's a saying that goes, **"Most people don't aim too high and miss, they aim too low and hit!"** If your goal is to get at least a C on your paper and you know you can do better, what's the challenge? If your goal is to do at least 25 sit-ups and you are already able to do 24 with no problem at all, what's the challenge?

And your goal must be your own. When you set a goal, *own* it. It has to be one that you yourself want. When someone else sets goals for you, you're not going to be very motivated toward achieving them. If your parents want you to be a good student, that's one thing. But if you want to be a good student, that's another. You are likely to be a good student because that's your goal, too. You have to have an inner fire, a drive that says, "This is important to ME."

One final point about desire. Alone, it is not enough. You might desire to grow wings and fly away, but can you? Of course not! If you set a goal that's just plain too difficult for you, you send the wrong pattern to your brain, a pattern that says goals cannot be accomplished. There's the ideal, and then there's the possible. If you want to memorize 300 words for the SAT (Scholastic Aptitude Test) and have one afternoon to do so, that's an ideal, but almost certainly impossible, goal. On the other hand, if you break up the words, memorizing 10 a day, that might be very hard, but possible. Strike a happy medium between No desire because the goal is too easy, and A lot of desire but no success because the goal is impossible.

2. Belief

You have to believe that you can meet your goals. In order to believe in the goal, the goal must be believable. That means that it must be achievable. Note that it doesn't have to be easy. But there has to be a better than 50-50 chance that you can meet the goal. You don't want a goal that's self-defeating, one that's so hard you almost certainly will not achieve it. Set a goal that you personally can achieve.

There is a direct relationship between how much you believe in a goal, and how quickly you achieve it. I often hear students complaining because their goals take forever to reach. There could be a few reasons for that, including that the goal is uncontrollable or illogical. But most often, the goal takes a long time to accomplish because the goal setter doesn't believe in it strongly enough. If you set a goal of learning to fix your car, but only read a few books on the subject because you don't really think you are a good enough mechanic to do the job, it's going to take you forever to fix it. On the other hand, if you sincerely believe in your goal, feel that you can learn to work on your car, that you can become a skilled mechanic, you're going to take a class, talk to other mechanics, and read those books. You're going to accomplish your goal a lot more quickly.

3. Writing

Write your goals down. When you write your goals down, you have to be clear about them in your mind. Writing down goals also keeps you organized. It makes you have a plan of attack: a beginning, middle, and end. The beginning is thinking of and writing down the goal, the middle is working toward it, and the end is accomplishing it.

There's another reason to write down a goal. You internalize—buy into—your commitment when you put pencil to paper. If you just think of your goal, you can forget about it as easily. We have hundreds of thousands of thoughts daily; most are forgotten in moments. But those we take the time and effort to write down seem to matter more. Suppose that you want to build a house, and you hire an architect. He meets with you and says, "I have a lot of great ideas. Here I am going to put the master bedroom with high ceilings; here I am going to put the jacuzzi; here I am going to put the swimming pool...." You listen for a while, then say, "I am having trouble remembering and visualizing all this. May I see your blueprints please?" The architect smiles at you and says, "Blueprints? I never write anything down. I keep it all in my head!" Ha! Are you going to let that person build your house, or are you going to get someone who has a plan he can put down on paper? Even if the architect is a genius, no one can work without a blueprint. The same is true for you and your goals. Writing them down gives you a blueprint for your efforts.

4. Benefits

What makes your goal worth achieving? It's natural for you to want to know what you're going to get out of something before you are willing to put in the time and effort. In other words, you want to know the benefits. When your teacher is lecturing, and she says, "Now, this next material will not be on the test, but you should know it anyway," what do you do? Do you sit there and pay as much attention as you normally would, or do you exchange a grin with your friends, sit back, and relax? Like most of us, you probably just kick back. You don't take the material seriously, because you know you won't be tested on it. You assume there is little benefit to you for taking notes and paying attention. So when you set a goal and begin working toward it, take a few minutes to think about what you're going to get out of accomplishing it. For example, suppose you want to get in shape. How many benefits can you think of? You will look better, maybe get more attention and more dates. You will feel better physically, maybe get stronger and be able to do better in sports. You will feel better emotionally, having more confidence and self-esteem. The more reasons you think of for achieving the goal, the stronger will be your desire. And, the stronger the desire, the easier it is to reach your goal.

5. Starting Point

You have to know where you are now in order to set a reasonable goal. For example, if you want to run 100 meters in a certain time, you need to find out your speed now so that you can begin your training program. If you want to get a good SAT score, take a diagnostic exam now to see what level you're at already, so you know how much and what material to study.

6. Deadlines

Set a deadline or date for completing your goal. You want to have a definite commitment to an ending point. Is your goal a long-term one, something like getting into a good college? Or is it a short-term one, like doing well on the exam next Tuesday? In many cases, the very best kind are long-term goals broken down into short-term goals. For example, getting into college is the long-term goal, an overall dream. But in order to reach that long-term goal, you need a lot of short-term goals, ranging from doing well in each of your classes to getting the money together for tuition. And goals and deadlines seem a lot easier to reach when they are broken down into manageable tasks.

Have dates for everything, major and minor. Now, some dates are set for you. If you are going to take the SAT college admission exam, for example, you know that you have to be prepared and have all your studying done by the date of the exam. But you can still set your intermediate deadlines: have the vocabulary learned by this date, the math by that date. Having a date written down motivates you. It also helps you prioritize where and how you will allocate (spend) your time. Then, if you know that you are nearing the deadline, you can push yourself just a little harder. And when you do accomplish your goal within the deadline, you feel like a winner.

A word of caution. Don't set overly ambitious deadlines. Don't say you are going to make 10 new friends this month if you're a very shy person who has trouble making 10 new friends a year. Don't say that by the end of this semester you are going to take 10 seconds off your sprint time if you have not taken off more than one second a semester so far. Set a realistic deadline. You can do just about anything you set your mind to, as long as you give yourself sufficient time to do so. You can pass your spelling test tomorrow if you take the time to study for it.

Rewarding Yourself

Let's say that you have gone through all the six steps. You have set a goal, and accomplished it. Now REWARD YOURSELF! You did something you set your mind to, and you deserve to be proud of yourself. What one nice thing will you do for yourself because you have been diligent and hard at work on your goal?

Maybe it's a few days of just "down time," or a new item of clothing, or tickets to a special concert. Think about the goal you listed earlier. What will your reward be?

When I accomplish the goal, my reward will be: _____

_____

EXERCISE 1. *What's Important to YOU?*

Turn back to page 17, where you chose your number one goal. Write your goal on the blank line entitled "Goal" on the next page. Now, go through the six steps of goal setting for that goal. An example is given below to help you get started.

Goal: To be a starter on the basketball team.

Desire: I have wanted to be a starter ever since I was in 7th grade. This is something I even daydream about.

Belief: I know that I am strong enough and have the skills to be a starter. I am almost as good as other starters already on the team. I know I can make it.

Writing: On an index card taped to my mirror at home, I have written, "Be a starter on the basketball team!"

Benefits: If I am a starter, I will get more playing time, will have more fun with my friends, get to practice with the really good players and thus improve myself. I will also get more respect, make my parents proud of me, and maybe get more dates. And it will look good on my transcript when I am ready to go to college.

Starting point: I know that I'm the best second-stringer on the basketball team. If something were to happen to a substitute for a varsity player, I would get the job. But I am almost as good as the last two starters on the team, so with just a little more work, I might be able to get one of their positions, even if they stay healthy and want to keep playing.

Deadline: I have to make starter by the third week of the semester. That's when the positions will be fixed. Coach says that he is loyal to his players, and that once the roles are assigned, he won't change them unless someone is sick or unable to play.

Now you try it.

Goal: _____

Desire: _____
_____

Belief: _____
_____

Writing: _____
_____

Benefits: _____
_____

Starting point: _____
_____

Deadline: _____
_____

EXERCISE 2. *Evaluating Your Goal*

Now that you have gone through the steps, go back and think about them a second time. Answer these questions for the goal you set.

1. Evaluate your goal. Is it clear? Is it specific? Does it conflict withother goals that are important to you? _____

   _____

2. How much you desire a goal often determines whether you achieve it. Be honest with yourself. Is this goal really what you want to be, to have, or to do? _____

   _____

3. Do you believe you can accomplish your goal? Do you have at least a 50 percent chance of achieving it? If not, rewrite the goal so that you do have a 50 percent chance of achieving it. _____

   _____

4. Did you put your goal in writing? Did you make a couple of copies to keep in front of you (one copy for your mirror, one for your notebook, etc.)? Where will you put them? _____

   _____

5. Why do you want to achieve this goal? What's in it for you? Remember, the more reasons you list, the more likely it is you'll achieve your goal. _____

   _____

6. Did you set a reasonable deadline? What are your chances of reaching your goal by the date you set? _____

_____

7. How can you keep from getting discouraged when you have a long way to go before reaching your goal? _____

_____

Exercise 3. *Setting Subgoals*

Breaking a goal into subgoals can help you know where to begin. Here's an example.

Major goal: GO TO COLLEGE

Subgoals

June: Take a tutoring course to prepare for the SAT

July: Take the SAT

September: Gather the necessary letters of recommendation.
    Research college choices.

October: Pick five colleges and get application forms.

November: Complete and mail college applications.

December: Apply for financial aid, etc.

Choose one of your goals and complete the following steps.

Your major goal: _____

Subgoals: _____

Chapter 4

Overcoming Obstacles to Achieving Goals

Earlier in this book, you learned some reasons or excuses people make for not setting goals. Those were obstacles to getting started in setting goals. But now you're going to go a step further. You've come up with a list of goals you really want to accomplish, and identified your Number One Goal. There are probably a few obstacles you have to overcome in order to achieve your goal. Here are six important steps that can help you reach your goals.

Six Steps on the Path to Success

1. Identify the Obstacles

If your goal is to be allowed to go on an overnight camping trip with your friends, the major obstacle might be that your mother has said you can't go. A second obstacle might be that you don't have the money for the trip. And a third obstacle might be that you have to spend that weekend studying for your History final exam. These odds might look overwhelming, but don't be discouraged! All goals have obstacles. The more obstacles you can identify, the easier it will be once you start to work toward accomplishing your goal.

2. Identify the Knowledge You Require

Okay, now you have set the goals and identified the obstacles. The next step is to find out what you need to know to overcome the obstacles. Think of it in terms of school. If you want to do well on the Spanish test, you have to identify what material is on the test, so you can study it. If the test is going to include irregular verbs, or the preterit, you have to know that to study. If you don't know what is on the exam, you might study all the wrong things. Even though your general knowledge is improved, that will be small comfort when you get back your exam with a D on it. And once you identify your gaps of knowledge, you have to go about ranking them in priority before you fill them. For example, before you begin driving, you may not know about road etiquette (manners among drivers), or about safety rules. Which is more important to know? Obviously, the safety rules. You have to find out what knowledge you need, then decide in which order you are going to acquire that knowledge.

3. Identify the People Who Can Help

The third step is to find out who can help you meet your goals. Suppose your goal is to get an athletic scholarship to college. The coach can help you meet that goal. You don't have to do everything by yourself. In fact, most of us feel terrific when we are able to help someone else. People are eager to do what they can to help you. When you run up against an obstacle, when you are setting a goal that seems hard to accomplish, identify your personal resources. Who can help you?

4. Make a Plan

You need to have a plan before you begin taking action, otherwise you'll waste a lot of time and resources and probably become extremely frustrated. Remember that architect who had no blueprint? He might start building without having the materials, without knowing what he's working on, and end up with a chicken coop when he was supposed to build a dog house. If you don't have a plan, you can make all sorts of mistakes. A plan is really a list of activities. Decide what you have to do. Try to think of every single step. Be as specific as possible. For example, if you want to win the science fair with your project, that's your goal. What activities can you take toward accomplishing that goal? Don't just say, "Build the best project." That's too vague. Be more specific. You can get several books on the subject. You can talk to others who have built projects like yours so that you know what problems they had and how they overcame them. You can begin gathering the materials you will need. You can get a commitment from your science teacher to spend time with you reviewing the project.

You can put together the actual project, then begin the paperwork. You can ask your older brother to type your report. When you first begin learning this planning skill, you may find that you can't think of very many things to write down in your plan. But as you get better and better, your plan will become more complete. And the more complete the plan, the easier it is to reach your goal. Once you have your list of activities, the next step is to *prioritize* them. Assign them levels of importance. Doing so lets you know where to begin your efforts.

5. Visualize

When you visualize something, you see it in your mind. You create a mental picture of yourself doing what you want to do. The subconscious does only what you tell it to do. If you consciously think of something, the subconscious will kick into gear and get busy doing the work you want it to do. Have you ever heard the expression, *"What you see is what you get?"* That summarizes visualization very well. If you see yourself working toward your goals and ultimately achieving them, that's exactly what will happen.

6. Be Determined and Persistent

If something is worth doing, if it's a goal, most likely it will not be all that easy to achieve. It takes determination to meet your goals, persistence to hang in there when things are rough. You can do whatever you set your mind to. Anticipate the difficulties, and never give up. Winston Churchill was asked one time what the secret of his success was, and he said it in just seven words: "Never give up. Never, never give up."

EXERCISE 1. *Accomplishing Your Goal*

1. Think of a goal you would like to accomplish, but that appears too difficult to obtain now. Choose one that seems to have a lot of obstacles in the way. Then go through these six steps and try to see how you could accomplish that goal. To help you do this, the goal from the previous chapter has been used.

   <u>Goal:</u> To be a starter on the basketball team.

   Identify the obstacles: All the starting positions are already filled. Even though I'm the best second-stringer on the team, I may not be able to improve enough to take over a starting position, especially if all the starters improve, too.

   Identify the knowledge you require: I need to know what the coach is looking for in starters. I need to know the most important thing for me to work on improving.

   Identify people who can help: The coach can tell me what he values most in a player. My friends can help by playing basketball with me when we get together, instead of watching movies. My parents can help me watch what I eat, and be understanding about my needing more free time for practice.

Make a plan: I need to make a workout schedule and stick to it. I need to get people involved in helping me reach my goal.

Visualize: I will see the crowd cheer as I make a block or score a basket.

Be determined and persistent: I won't get discouraged. I'll concentrate on being the best player I can be.

Now you try it.

Goal: _____

Identify the obstacles: _____
_____

Identify the knowledge you require: _____
_____

Identify the people who can help: _____
_____

Make a plan: _____
_____

Visualize: _____
_____

Be determined and persistent: _____
_____

EXERCISE 2. *Overcoming Obstacles*

1. Review the obstacles to your goal. Can you think of any others? _____
   _____

2. You have identified the knowledge you require, and determined how you are going to get it. Is your plan realistic? _____
   _____

3. You have identified people you want to help you. Have you chosen people who are qualified to help you? Will they be willing to help? _____
   _____

4. Review your plan. Does it overcome all the obstacles you listed above? Is it realistic and workable? Be sure to set priorities and mini-deadlines in your plan. _____
   _____

5. How will you visualize yourself succeeding? _____
   _____

6. How determined are you to accomplish this goal? Resolve to reach this goal, no matter what. How can you make the commitment to persist? _____
   _____

Chapter 5

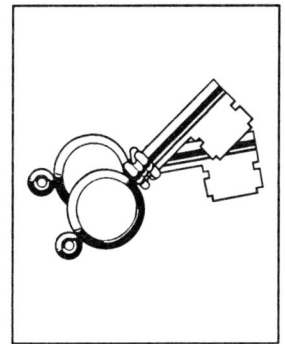

The Keys to Success

Would you prefer to be happy or sad, popular or unpopular, a success or a failure? Of course you'd prefer to be happy, popular, and successful. The good news is—it's easy to be all those things! You can choose how you want your life to be! Here are six keys to making your choices work.

The Six Keys to Success

1. Peace of Mind

Peace of mind is a key element of success. Peace of mind is being free from worry. You have it when you go to bed at night and can lie there peacefully, rather than worry. You have it when you know you have done your best and can be content with that. When you are doing well in your relationships, goals and work (school, job, athletics, etc.), you have peace of mind. However, when you're doing well in school, but aren't getting along with your parents, you probably won't have peace of mind. Your peace of mind will be greatest when you find balance in your life (personal, scholastic and social).

2. Health and Energy

Successful people are generally healthy and have a high level of energy. They value their health. They know you need to be healthy and energetic to do the things required to become a success. And, feeling successful can make you more energetic. Once you experience success, you become more energized, willing to work even harder.

3. Loving Relationships

If you want to be successful, you need to focus on all of the things in your life: school, friendships, peace of mind, work, family, etc. Some people think of success as having an expensive house, a fancy car, and a lot of money. Although these things certainly are nice to have, they seem less significant if your dad or mom doesn't love you, or if you have very few friends. The recognition and admiration and love of our friends and family are very important to all of us. And good relationships make our lives better.

4. Financial Freedom

Financial success is a worthy goal; it's perfectly okay to want money, to enjoy money. It can't be the whole focus of your life, of course, but earning enough money is important because of what it represents: financial freedom. And that's important. Your parents don't want to worry about where the next meal is coming from or how they're going to pay the rent. They need to be financially secure so that each month they can pay these bills without pressure.

Perhaps you know of others who have convinced themselves that acquiring masses of money and the material things money can buy signifies the achievement of success and status. They think that they can gain respect by owning more things than those around them. But this isn't true. That's why so many who seek happiness through material wealth are wanting and unsatisfied. It's not money, but rather what it can do that's important. Just having money or material possessions is not enough. Knowledge, achievement, and personal satisfaction are also indicators of wealth. So you see, money is all relative. No one else can tell you the amount you need. You know how much money you need to feel successful and to live a certain lifestyle. But it's hard to feel successful if you have no money at all. If you have great ideas for solving world hunger, but you have to keep worrying about how to pay the rent, how much effort are you going to be able to put into your other projects? The freedom that money represents is an essential element of success. You need to think about money, and how you will go about earning enough for the life you want to build.

5. Worthy Goals and Ideals

It's hard to think of yourself as a success unless you work toward something worthwhile. "Worthwhile" means something different to everyone. Maybe you think that worthwhile means you have to earn a lot of money, become a rabbi, or a doctor, or earn a Ph.D. degree. But it doesn't have to be just career accomplishments. You do something worthwhile when you are nicer to your little brother. You do something worthwhile by being a caring son, daughter, friend, or student.

Sometimes you have to change your ideals in order to be a success, to feel you are making the most of your potential. At first, you may go too far when determining your ideals. For example, maybe you decide that being smart is the most important thing in the world—you make good grades and think you are successful, but no one likes you. So you reevaluate your life and decide that being popular is more important than being smart. You become nice, treat others better. And, to your surprise, you still get good grades. At first, you may slip from a B to a C in one or two classes, but in time your overall GPA stays where you want it to. You have found a balance when you realize you can be both smart and popular. That gives you the best of both situations. You still make good grades, but because you worked harder at being nicer to others, helping them when they were having a rough time, they like you more. You change from a limiting ideal to a worthy one.

6. Personal Fulfillment

When you do what you enjoy, what you feel you are meant to do, and do it well, you experience personal fulfillment. Personal fulfillment means your life is on the right track, everything seems to be running smoothly. It's that warm feeling that says you are doing your best. That doesn't have to be *the* best, just *your* best. For example, maybe after a lot of practice, you lowered your sprint time, or raised your Math score. Even if you're not the quickest runner on the team or the top mathematician in the class, you did your best and are happy. **Ultimately, you have only one critic to satisfy, and that's the hardest one: yourself.**

EXERCISE 1. *Defining Success for YOU*

1. See how you can apply these keys to your own life. Choose one person you know who appears to be successful. Now, go through the six keys to success again. For each key, write an example of how it is used by the successful person you listed. An example will help you get started.

    Successful Person: My brother Kevin

    Peace of Mind: He rarely seems to worry and is usually cheerful. If he fails at something, he shrugs, and says, "Well, I did my very best and I can't ask anything more than that of myself."

Health and Energy: Kevin is an athlete, working out at the gym a couple of times a week. He takes care of himself, eating right and getting enough sleep. And he always seems to keep going when the rest of us are tired and ready to give up.

Loving Relationships: Kevin doesn't have a girlfriend right now, but he has a lot of good friends he talks to every day, and with whom he does all sorts of fun activities. He is close to me and the rest of our family, and knows we will help him out if he needs us.

Financial Freedom: Kevin has a part-time job at a fast-food place. He makes enough money to date and to take care of his car. He is putting a little money away for college. Although he doesn't have as much money as he'd like and has to be careful about saving, he's never broke.

Worthy Goals and Ideals: Kevin wants to get a good job after college and make enough money to send our parents to Hawaii for their twenty-fifth wedding anniversary. He also wants to get involved in politics and maybe even run for office to do what he can to improve the community.

Personal Fulfillment: Kevin likes himself. He never seems too shy to ask out a girl or to be fixed up on a blind date, because he is comfortable being himself.

Now you try it.

Successful Person: _____

_____

Peace of Mind: _____

_____

Health and Energy: _____

_____

Loving Relationships: _____

_____

Financial Freedom: _____

_____

Worthy Goals and Ideals: _____

_____

Personal Fulfillment: _____

_____

EXERCISE 2. *Goals for YOUR Success*

1. These six keys can work for you. But you have to make the commitment to apply the keys to your own life. What steps can you take toward using each key in your own life? An example is given to help you get started.

    Peace of Mind: I will keep assuring myself that I am doing my best, will give myself a break and not expect perfection. The next time I make a mistake, I will forgive myself.

    Health and Energy: I will start eating the right foods, cutting back on junk foods. I will get more exercise and enough sleep.

    Loving Relationships: I will spend more time with my family and show them how much I care about them. I will think about my friends' feelings more and let them know I'm glad we're friends. When I'm depressed, I will not hesitate to let my family and friends help me.

    Financial Freedom: I will keep track of where my money goes, marking down what I spend it on. Then I will analyze that list, and resolve to stop wasting money. I will try to save a little of my allowance, or the paycheck from my part-time job, so that there will always be a little money in the bank in case there is something special I want.

Worthy Goals and Ideals: I will think of what I can do to make life better for my family and friends and for everyone around me. I will try to do at least one nice thing for someone else every time I do one nice thing for myself.

Personal Fulfillment: I will count my blessings! I will note how lucky I am to be healthy and loved and to have friends. I will think about how terrific my life is, and the good things about being me.

Now you try it.

Peace of Mind: _____
_____
_____

Health and Energy: _____
_____
_____

Loving Relationships: _____
_____
_____

Financial Freedom: _____
_____
_____

Worthy Goals and Ideals: _____

_____

_____

Personal Fulfillment: _____

_____

_____

Daily Goal Setting

Each night before going to sleep, review your five uppermost values in life and five exciting lifetime goals. Determine in order of priority the six most important things you want to do in the next day that will move you with purpose to a more effective and productive day. Keep a 3 x 5 card to review.

My Uppermost Values in Life Are:

1. _____

2. _____

3. _____

4. _____

5. _____

Five Exciting Lifetime Goals:

1. _____

2. _____

3. _____

4. _____

5. _____

Make a daily "TO DO" list on a 3 x 5 card:

TO DO: Date:

1. _____

2. _____

3. _____

4. _____

5. _____

6. _____

Remember, If You Don't Know Where You're Going You May End Up Somewhere Else!

WEEKLY GOALS

WEEK: _____   PRIORITY

#1 _____   _____
   _____

#2 _____   _____
   _____

#3 _____   _____
   _____

#4 _____   _____
   _____

Must remember to do: _____   _____
_____

Special events this week: _____   _____
_____

Special needs: _____   _____
_____

MONTHLY GOALS

WEEK:_____   PRIORITY

#1 _____   _____
   _____

#2 _____   _____
   _____

#3 _____   _____
   _____

#4 _____   _____
   _____

Must remember to do: _____   _____
_____

Special events this month: _____   _____
_____

Special needs: _____   _____
_____

Order NOW 10% Discount On 3 Or More Titles!

20+ YEARS AWARD WINNING PUBLISHER

At Last... You Can Be That
"MOST MEMORABLE" PARENT/TEACHER/CARE-GIVER
To Every Person Whose Life You Touch (Including Your Own!)

HELP KIDS TO: ❖ IMPROVE GRADES ❖ INCREASE CLASS PARTICIPATION ❖ BECOME MORE ATTENTIVE
ENCOURAGE & INSPIRE THEM AND YOU TO: ❖ TACKLE PROBLEMS ❖ ACHIEVE GOALS
AND
IMPROVE SELF-ESTEEM — BOTH THEIRS AND YOURS

Our authors are not just writers, but researchers and practitioners. Our books are not just written, but proven effective. All 100% tested, 100% practical, 100% effective. Look over our titles, choose the ones you want, and send your order today. You'll be glad you did. Just remember, our books are "SIMPLY THE BEST." — Bradley L. Winch, Ph.D., JD — President and Publisher

---

Sandy Mc Daniel & Peggy Bielen

Project Self-Esteem, Expanded (Gr. K-8)

Innovative *parent involvement program.* Used by over 2000 schools/400,000 participants. Teaches children to respect themselves and others, make sound decisions, honor personal and family value systems, develop vocabulary, attitude, goals and behavior needed for *living successfully*, *practicing responsible behavior* and *avoiding drug and alcohol use.* VHS, 1½ hrs. $149.95

0-915190-59-1, 408 pages, **JP-9059-1 $39.95**
8½ x 11, paperback, illus., reprod. act. sheets

Esteem Builders (Gr. K-8)

Teach self-esteem via curriculum content. Best K-8 program available. Uses 5 building blocks of self-esteem (*security/ selfhood/affiliation/mission/ competence*) as base. Over 250 grade level/curric. content cross-correlated activities. Also assess. tool, checklist of educator behaviors for modeling, 40 week lesson planner, ext. bibliography and more.

Paperback, 464 pages, **JP-9053-2 $39.95**
Spiral bound, **JP-9088-5 $49.95**, 8½ x 11, illus.

Michele Borba, Ed.D.

NOT JUST AUTHORS BUT RESEARCHERS AND PRACTITIONERS.

![Naomi Drew book cover]

Naomi Drew, M.A.

Learning The Skills of Peacemaking: Communicating/Cooperation/Resolving Conflict (Gr. K-8)

Help kids say "No" to fighting. Establish WIN/WIN guidelines for conflicts in your classroom. *Over fifty lessons*: peace begins with me; integrating peacemaking into our lives; exploring our roots and interconnectedness. Great for *self-esteem* and *cultural diversity* programs.

0-915190-46-X, 224 pages, **JP-9046-X $21.95**
8½ x 11, paperback, illus., reprod. act. sheets

6 Vital Ingredients of Self-Esteem: How To Develop Them In Your Students (Gr. K-12)

Put self-esteem to work for your students. Learn practical ways to help kids manage school, make decisions, accept consequences, manage time, and discipline themselves to set worthwhile goals...and much more. *Covers developmental stages from ages 2 to 18, with implications for self-esteem at each stage.*

0-915190-72-9, 192 pages, **JP-9072-9 $19.95**
8½ x 11, paperback, biblio., appendices

Bettie B. Youngs, Ph.D.

NOT JUST WRITTEN BUT PROVEN EFFECTIVE.

![You & Self Esteem book cover]

Bettie B. Youngs, Ph.D.

You & Self-Esteem: The Key To Happiness & Success (Gr. 5-12)

Comprehensive *workbook* for young people. Defines *self-esteem* and its importance in their lives; helps them identify why and how it adds or detracts from their vitality; shows them how to protect it from being shattered by others; outlines a *plan of action* to keep their self-esteem *positive.* Very useful. Companion to *6 Vital Ingredients*.

0-915190-83-4, 160 pages, **JP-9083-4 $16.95**
8½ x 11, paperback, biblio., appendices

Partners for Change: Peer Helping Guide For Training and Prevention (Gr. K-12)

This comprehensive *program guide* provides an excellent *peer support program* for program coordinators, peer leaders, professionals, group homes, churches, social agencies and schools. *Covers 12 areas,* including suicide, HIV / Aids, child abuse, teen pregnancy, substance abuse, low self esteem, dropouts, child abduction. etc.

Paperback, 464 pages, **JP-9069-9 $44.95**
Spiral bound, **JP-9087-7 $49.95**, 8½ x 11, illus.

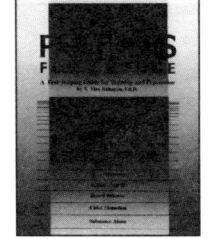

V. Alex Kehayan, Ed.D.

100% TESTED — 100% PRACTICAL — 100% GUARANTEED.

V. Alex Kehayan, Ed.D.

Self-Awareness Growth Experiences (Gr. 7-12)

Over *593 strategies/activities* covering affective learning goals and objectives. To increase: self-awareness/self-esteem/social interaction skills/problem-solving, decision-making skills/coping ability /ethical standards/independent functioning/ creativity. Great *secondary resource*. Useful in counseling situations.

0-915190-61-3, 224 pages, **JP-9061-3 $16.95**
6 x 9, paperback, illus., 593 activities

Unlocking Doors to Self-Esteem (Gr. 7-12)

Contains *curriculum content objectives with underlying social objectives.* Shows how to teach both at the same time. *Content objectives* in English/Drama/Social Science/Career Science/Physical Education. *Social objectives* in Developing Positive Self-Concepts/Examining Attitudes, Feelings and Actions/Fostering Positive Relationships.

0-915190-60-5, 224 pages, **JP-9060-5 $16.95**
6 x 9, paperback, illus., 100 lesson plans

C. Lynn Fox, Ph.D. & Francine L. Weaver, M.A.

ORDER FROM: B.L. Winch & Associates/Jalmar Press, Skypark Business Center, 2675 Skypark Drive, Suite 204, Torrance, CA 90505
CALL TOLL FREE — (800) 662-9662 • (310) 784-0016 • FAX (310) 784-1379 • Add 10% shipping; $3 minimum

6/95

Order NOW 10% Discount On 3 Or More Titles!

DISCOVER materials for positive self-esteem.
CREATE a positive environment in your classroom or home by opening a world of understanding.

20+ YEARS AWARD WINNING PUBLISHER

Esther Wright, M.A.

Good Morning Class - I Love You (Staff)

Contains thought provoking quotes and questions about *teaching from the heart*. Helps love become an integral part of the learning that goes on in every classroom. Great for new teachers and for experienced teachers who sometimes become frustrated by the system. Use this book to begin and end your day. Greet your students every day with: *"Good morning class - I love you."*

0-915190-58-3, 80 pages, **JP-9058-3 $7.95**
5½ x 8½, paperback, illus./ **Button $1.50**

Enhancing Educator's Self-Esteem: It's Criteria #1 (Staff)

For the educator, a *healthy self-esteem* is job criterion No. 1! When high, it empowers us and adds to the vitality of our lives; when low it saps energy, erodes our confidence, lowers productivity and blocks our initiative to care about self and others. Follow the *plan of action* in this great resource to develop your self-esteem.

0-915190-79-6, 144 pages, **JP-9079-6 $16.95**
8½ x 11, paperback

Bettie B. Youngs, Ph.D.

NOT JUST AUTHORS BUT RESEARCHERS AND PRACTITIONERS.

Elaine Young, M.A. with R. Frelow, Ph.D.

I Am a Blade of Grass (Staff)

Create a school where all — students, teachers, administrators, and parents — see themselves as both learners and leaders *in partnership*. Develop a new *compact for learning* that focuses on results, that promotes *local initiative* and that empowers people at all levels of the system. How to in this *collaborative curriculum*. Great for self-esteem.

0-915190-54-0, 176 pages, **JP-9054-0 $14.95**
6 x 9, paperback, illustrations

Stress Management for Educators: A Guide to Manage Our Response to Stress (Staff)

Answers these significant questions for educators: *What is stress? What causes it? How do I cope with it? What can be done to manage stress to moderate its negative effects? Can stress be used to advantage? How can educators be stress-proofed* to help them remain at *peak performance?* How do I keep going in spite of it?

0-915190-77-X, 112 pages, **JP-9077-X $12.95**
8½ x 11, paperback, illus., charts

Bettie B. Youngs, Ph.D.

NOT JUST WRITTEN BUT PROVEN EFFECTIVE.

Eva D. Fugitt, M.A.

He Hit Me Back First: Self-Esteem Through Self-Discipline (Gr. K-8)

By whose authority does a child choose right from wrong? Here are *activities* directed toward *developing* within the child an *awareness* of his own *inner authority* and ability to choose (will power) and the resulting sense of *responsibility*, *freedom* and *self-esteem*. 29 separate activities.

0-915190-64-8, 120 pages, **JP-9064-8 $12.95**
8½ x 11, paperback, appendix, biblio.

Let's Get Together! (Gr. K-6)

Making friends is *easy* with the activities in this thoroughly researched book. Students are paired, get to know about each other, produce a book about their new *friend*, and present it in class. Exciting activities help discover commonalities. Great *self-esteem booster*. Revised after 10 years of field testing. Over 150 activities in 18 lessons.

0-915190-75-3, 192 pages, **JP-9075-3 $19.95**
8½ x 11, paperback, illustrations, activities

C. Lynn Fox, Ph.D.

100% TESTED — 100% PRACTICAL — 100% GUARANTEED.

Chris Schriner, Rel.D.

Feel Better Now: 30 Ways to Handle Frustration in Three Minutes or Less (Staff/Personal)

Teaches people to *handle stress as it happens* rapidly and directly. This basic requirement for *emotional survival* and *physical health* can be learned with the methods in this book. Find your own recipe for relief. Foreword: Ken Keyes, Jr. *"A mine of practical help"* — says Rev. Robert Schuller.

0-915190-66-4, 180 pages, **JP-9066-4 $9.95**
6 x 9, paperback, appendix, bibliography

Peace in 100 Languages: A One-Word Multilingual Dictionary (Staff/Personal)

A candidate for the Guinness Book of World Records, it is the *largest/smallest dictionary ever published*. Envisioned, researched and developed by *Russian peace activists*. Ancient, national, local and special languages covered. A portion of purchase price will be donated to joint U.S./Russian peace project.

0-915190-74-5, 48 pages, **JP-9074-5 $9.95**
5 x 10, glossy paperback, full color

By:
M. Kabattchenko,
V. Kochurov,
L. Koshanova,
E. Kononenko,
D. Kuznetsov,
A. Lapitsky,
V. Monakov,
L. Stoupin, and
A. Zagorsky

ORDER NOW FOR 10% DISCOUNT ON 3 OR MORE TITLES.

NEW

Gordon Dryden, Jeannette Vos, Ed.D.

The Learning Revolution (Adult)

A revolution is changing your life and your world. Here's a book that tells how this revolution is taking shape in America and how it can give us the world's best educational system by the year 2000. That revolution is gathering speed -- a revolution that can help us learn anything five times faster, better, and easier. A must reading for parents, teachers and business people.

1-880396-34-3, 528 pages, **JP9634-3 $29.95**
6 x 9, hard-cover, many quotes, biblio.

Hilde Knows: Someone Cries for the Children (Staff/Personal)

We're all aware of the growing problem of child abuse. In this book, a dashshund, is kidnapped from her happy family. The dog sees child abuse firsthand, when the parents abuse their daughter. Psychiatrist Dr. Machlin, outlines how caring adults can use the book with a child.

1-880396-38-6, 48 pages, **JP9638-6 $6.95**
7 x 8½, fully illustrated

NEW

Lisa Kent
Illust. by Mikki Machlin

ORDER FROM: B.L. Winch & Associates/Jalmar Press, Skypark Business Center, 2675 Skypark Drive, Suite 204, Torrance, CA 90505
CALL TOLL FREE — (800) 662-9662 • (310) 784-0016 • FAX (310) 784-1379 • Add 10% shipping; $3 minimum

6/95

Order NOW 10% Discount On 3 Or More Titles!

DISCOVER books on self-esteem for kids.
ENJOY great reading with Warm Fuzzies and Squib, the adventurous owl.

20+ YEARS AWARD WINNING PUBLISHER

Larry Shles, M.A.

Moths & Mothers/Feathers & Fathers: The Story of Squib, The Owl, Begins (Ages 5-105)

Heartwarming story of a tiny owl who cannot fly or hoot as he learns to put words with his feelings. He faces frustration, grief, fear, guilt and loneliness in his life, just as we do. Struggling with these *feelings*, he searches, at least, for *understanding*. *Delightfully illustrated*. Ageless.

0-915190-57-5, 72 pages, **JP-9057-5 $7.95**
8½ x 11, paperback, illustrations

Hoots & Toots & Hairy Brutes: The Continuing Adventures of Squib, The Owl (Ages 5-105)

Squib, who can only toot, sets out to learn how to give a mighty hoot. Even the *owl-odontist* can't help and he fails completely. Every reader who has struggled with *life's limitations* will recognize his own *struggles* and *triumphs* in the microcosm of Squib's forest world. A parable for all ages.

0-915190-56-7, 72 pages, **JP-9056-7 $7.95**
8½ x 11, paperback, illustrations

Larry Shles, M.A.

NOT JUST AUTHORS BUT RESEARCHERS AND PRACTITIONERS.

Larry Shles, M.A.

Hugs & Shrugs: The Continuing Saga of Squib, The Owl (Ages 5-105)

Squib feels *lonely, depressed* and *incomplete*. His reflection in the pond shows that he has lost a piece of himself. He thinks his missing piece fell out and he searches in vain outside of himself to find it. Only when he discovers that it fell in and not out does he *find inner-peace* and *become whole*. Delightfully illustrated. Ageless.

0-915190-47-8, 72 pages, **JP-9047-8 $7.95**
8½ x 11, paperback, illustrations

Aliens in my Nest: Squib Meets the Teen Creature (Ages 5-105)

What does it feel like to face a snarly, surly, defiant and non-communicative older brother turned *adolescent*? Friends, dress code, temperament, entertainment, room decor, eating habits, authority, music, isolation, *internal and external conflict* and many other *areas of change* are *dealt with*. Explores how to handle every situation.

0-915190-49-4, 80 pages, **JP-9049-4 $7.95**
8½ x 11, paperback, illustrations

Larry Shles, M.A.

NOT JUST WRITTEN BUT PROVEN EFFECTIVE.

Larry Shles, M.A.

Do I Have to Go to School Today? Squib Measures Up! (Ages 5-105)

Squib *dreads* going to *school*. He day-dreams about all the reasons he has not to go: the school bus will swallow him, the older kids will be mean to him, numbers and letters confuse him, he is too small for sports, etc. But, in the end, he *goes because his teacher accepts him "just as he is."* Very esteeming. Great metaphor for all ages.

0-915190-62-1, 64 pages, **JP-9062-1 $7.95**
8½ x 11, paperback, illustrations

**Scooter's Tail of Terror
A Fable of Addiction and Hope (Ages 5-105)**

Well-known author and illustrator, Larry Shles, introduces a new forest character — a squirrel named Scooter. He faces the challenge of addiction, but is offered a way to overcome it. As with the Squib books, the story is *simple*, yet the message is *dramatic*. The story touches the child within each reader and *presents the realities of addiction*.

0-915190-89-3, 80 pages, **JP-9089-3 $9.95**
8½ x 11, paperback, illustrations

Larry Shles, M.A.

100% TESTED — 100% PRACTICAL — 100% GUARANTEED.

REVISED

Alvyn Freed, Ph.D.

TA for Tots (and other prinzes) Revised (Gr. PreK-3)

Over 500,000 sold. New upright format. Book has helped thousands of young *children* and their *parents* to better *understand* and *relate to each other*. Helps youngsters realize their *intrinsic worth* as human beings; builds and strengthens their *self-esteem*. *Simple* to understand.
Coloring Book $1.95 / I'm OK Poster $3

0-915190-73-7, 144 pages, **JP-9073-7 $14.95**
8½ x 11, paperback, delightful illustrations

TA for Kids (and grown-ups too) (Gr. 4-9)

Over 250,000 sold. An ideal book to help youngsters *develop self-esteem*, esteem of others, *personal and social responsibility*, critical thinking and independent judgment. Book recognizes that each person is a unique human being with the capacity to learn, grow and develop. Hurray for TA! Great for parents and other care givers.

0-915190-09-5, 112 pages, **JP-9009-5 $9.95**
8½ x 11, paperback, illustrations

Alvyn Freed, Ph.D. & Margaret Freed

ORDER NOW FOR 10% DISCOUNT ON 3 OR MORE TITLES.

Alvyn Freed, Ph.D.

TA for Teens (and other important people) (Gr. 8-12)

Over 100,000 sold. The book that tells teenagers they're OK! Provides help in growing into adulthood in a mixed-up world. Contrasts freedom and irresponsibility with knowing that *youth need the skill, determination* and *inner strength* to reach *fulfillment* and *self-esteem*. No talking down to kids, here.

0-915190-03-6, 258 pages, **JP-9003-6 $21.95**
8½ x 11, paperback, illustrations

The Original Warm Fuzzy Tale (Gr. Pre K-Adult)

Over 100,000 sold. The concept of Warm Fuzzies and Cold Pricklies originated in this delightful story. A *fairy tale* in every sense, *with* adventure, fantasy, heroes, villians and a *moral*. Children (and adults, too) will enjoy this beautifully illustrated book.

0-915190-08-7, 48 pages, **JP-9008-7 $8.95**
6 x 9, paperback, full color illustrations

Claude Steiner, Ph.D

ORDER FROM: B.L. Winch & Associates/Jalmar Press, Skypark Business Center, 2675 Skypark Drive, Suite 204, Torrance, CA 90505
CALL TOLL FREE — (800) 662-9662 • (310) 784-0016 • FAX (310) 784-1379 • Add 10% shipping; $3 minimum

Order NOW 10% Discount On 3 Or More Titles!

OPEN your mind to wholebrain thinking and creative parenting.
GROW by leaps and bounds with our new ways to think and learn.

20+ YEARS AWARD WINNING PUBLISHER

Bob Samples, M.A.

Openmind/Wholemind: Parenting and Teaching Tomorrow's Children Today (Staff/Personal)

Can we learn to *treat* the *brain/mind system* as *open* rather than closed? Can we learn to *use all* our *learning modalities, learning styles, creativities* and *intelligences* to create a product far greater than the sum of its parts? Yes! This primer for parents and teachers shows how.

0-915190-45-1, 272 pages, **JP-9045-1 $14.95**
7 x 10, paperback, 81 B/W photos, illust.

Unicorns Are Real: A Right-Brained Approach to Learning (Gr. K-Adult)

Over 100,000 sold. The *alternate methods* of *teaching/learning* developed by the author have helped literally thousands of children and adults with *learning difficulties*. A book of *simple ideas* and *activities* that are easy to use, yet dramatically effective. Video of techniques also available: **VHS, 1½ hrs., JP-9113-0 $149.95. Unicorn Poster $4.95.**

0-915190-35-4, 144 pages, **JP-9035-4 $12.95**
8½ x 11, paperback, illus., assessment

Barbara Meister Vitale, M.A.

NOT JUST AUTHORS BUT RESEARCHERS AND PRACTITIONERS.

REVISED

Bob Samples, M.A.

Metaphoric Mind: A Celebration of Creative Consciousness (Revised) (Staff/Personal)

A plea for a balanced way of thinking and being in a culture that stands on the knife-edge between *catastrophe* and *transformation*. The metaphoric mind is *asking again, quietly but insistently, for equilibrium*. For, after all, equilibrium is the way of nature. A revised version of a classic.

0-915190-68-0, 208 pages, **JP-9068-0 $16.95**
7 x 9, paperback, B/W photos, illus.

Free Flight: Celebrating Your Right Brain (Staff/Personal)

Journey with Barbara Meister Vitale, from her uncertain childhood perceptions of being *"different"* to the acceptance and adult celebration of that difference. A how to *book for right-brained people in a left-brained world.* Foreword by Bob Samples- *"This book is born of the human soul."* Great gift item for your right-brained friends.

0-915190-44-3, 128 pages, **JP-9044-3 $9.95**
5½ x 8½, paperback, illustrations

Barbara Meister Vitale, M.A.

NOT JUST WRITTEN BUT PROVEN EFFECTIVE.

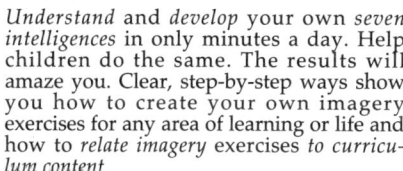

Lane Longino Waas, Ph.D.

Imagine That! Getting Smarter Through Imagery Practice (Gr. K-Adult)

Understand and *develop* your own *seven intelligences* in only minutes a day. Help children do the same. The results will amaze you. Clear, step-by-step ways show you how to create your own imagery exercises for any area of learning or life and how to *relate imagery exercises to curriculum content*

0-915190-71-0, 144 pages, **JP-9071-0 $12.95**
6 x 9, paperback, 42 B/W photos, biblio.

Becoming Whole (Learning) Through Games (Gr. K-Adult)

New ideas for old games. *Develop* your *child's brain power, motivation* and *self-esteem by playing*. An excellent parent/teacher guide and skills checklist to 100 standard games. Included are auditory, visual, motor, directional, modality, attention, educational, social and memory skills. Great resource for care givers.

0-915190-70-2, 288 pages, **JP-9070-2 $16.95**
6 x 9, paperback, glossary, biblio.

Gwen Bailey Moore, Ph.D. & Todd Serby

100% TESTED — 100% PRACTICAL — 100% GUARANTEED.

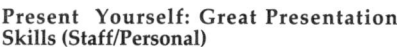

Michael J. Gelb, M.A.

Present Yourself: Great Presentation Skills (Staff/Personal)

Use *mind mapping* to become a presenter who is a dynamic part of the message. Learn about transforming fear, knowing your audience, setting the stage, making them remember and much more. *Essential reading* for anyone interested in *communication*. This book will become the standard work in its field. **Hardback, JP-9050-8 $16.95**

0-915190-51-6, 128 pages, **JP-9051-6 $9.95**
6 x 9, paperback, illus., mind maps

The Two Minute Lover (Staff/Personal)

With wit, wisdom and compassion, "The Two-Minute Lovers" and their proteges guide you through the steps of *building* and *maintaining* an *effective relationship* in a *fast-paced world*. They offer encouragement, inspiration and practical techniques for living happily in a relationship, even when outside pressures are enormous. Done like the "One Minute Manager".

0-915190-52-4, 112 pages, **JP-9052-4 $9.95**
6 x 9, paperback, illustrations

Asa Sparks, Ph.D.

ORDER NOW FOR 10% DISCOUNT ON 3 OR MORE TITLES.

James E. Gardner, Ph.D.

The Turbulent Teens: Understanding Helping, Surviving (Parents/Counselors)

Come to grips with the difficult issues of rules and the limits of parental tolerance, recognizing the necessity for *flexibility* that takes into consideration changes in the adolescent as well as the imperative *need for control*, agreed upon *expectations* and *accountability*. A must read! Useful in counseling situations.

0-913091-01-4, 224 pages, **JP-9101-4 $8.95**
6 x 9, paperback, case histories

The Parent Book: Raising Emotionally Mature Children - Ages 3-15 (Parents)

Improve *positive bonding* with your child in five easy steps: *listen* to the feelings; *learn* the basic concern; *develop* an action plan; *confront* with support; *spend* 1 to 1 time. Ideas for helping in 4 *self-esteem* related areas: *awareness; relating; competence; integrity*. 69 sub-catagories. Learn what's missing and what to do about it.

0-915190-15-X, 208 pages, **JP-9015-X $9.95**
8½ x 11, paperback, illus., diag/Rx.

Harold Besell, Ph.D. & Thomas P. Kelly, Jr.

ORDER FROM: B.L. Winch & Associates/Jalmar Press, Skypark Business Center, 2675 Skypark Drive, Suite 204, Torrance, CA 90505
CALL TOLL FREE — (800) 662-9662 • (310) 784-0016 • FAX (310) 784-1379 • Add 10% shipping; $3 minimum

6/95